NEW YORK GIANTS

BY BARRY WILNER

The Child's World

Published by The Child's World®
1980 Lookout Drive • Mankato, MN 56003-1705
800-599-READ • www.childsworld.com

Acknowledgments
The Child's World®: Mary Berendes, Publishing Director
Red Line Editorial: Editorial direction
The Design Lab: Design
Amnet: Production

Design Element: Dean Bertoncelj/Shutterstock Images
Photographs ©: Bill Kostroun/AP Images, cover; Rich
Kane/Icon Sportswire, 5, 25; AP Images, 7; Bettmann/
Corbis, 9, 19; Joe Robbins/AP Images, 11; Anthony
Quintano CC 2.0, 13; Aaron M. Sprecher/AP Images, 14–15;
Ed Reinke/AP Images, 17; Jeffrey Phelps/AP Images, 21;
Cliff Welch/Icon Sportswire, 23; Anthony J. Causi/Icon
Sportswire, 27; J.L. Dykstra/Icon Sportswire, 29

ISBN 9781634070041
LCCN 2014959709

Printed in the United States of America
Mankato, MN
July, 2015
PA02265

ABOUT THE AUTHOR

Barry Wilner has written 41 books, including many for young readers. He is a sports writer for The Associated Press and has covered such events as the Super Bowl, Olympics, and World Cup. He lives in Garnerville, New York.

TABLE OF CONTENTS

GO, GIANTS!

The New York Giants are one of the oldest teams in football. They started playing in 1925. Three other teams started playing that season, too. But the Giants are the only one left. They quickly became one of the best teams. That is still the case. Fans have watched New York win eight titles. Let's meet the Giants.

Defensive end Jason Pierre-Paul celebrates after tackling Arizona Cardinals quarterback Drew Stanton on September 14, 2014.

WHO ARE THE GIANTS?

The New York Giants play in the National Football **League** (NFL). They are one of the 32 teams in the NFL. The NFL includes the American Football Conference (AFC) and the National Football Conference (NFC). The winner of the NFC plays the winner of the AFC in the **Super Bowl**. The Giants play in the East Division of the NFC. The Giants won four NFL Championship Games in their first 41 seasons. They have won four more titles since the Super Bowl began after the 1966 season.

Quarterback Phil Simms throws a pass in the Super Bowl on January 25, 1987.

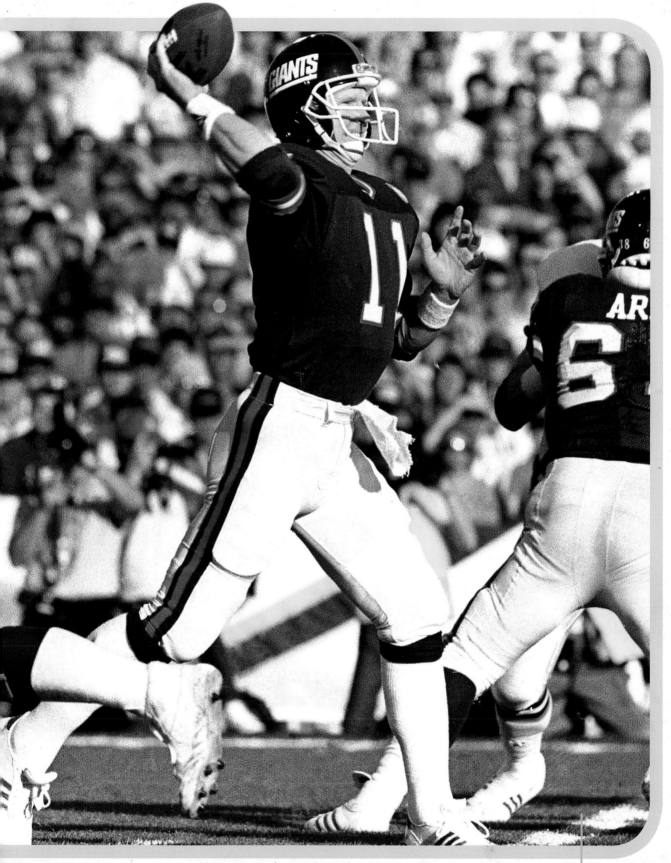

WHERE THEY CAME FROM

Tim Mara was the team's first owner. He paid $500 to start the Giants in 1925. At first, the team shared a stadium with the New York Giants baseball team. Mara used the same nickname for the football squad. The Giants barely stayed in business that first season. But then football's best player, Red Grange, came to town. He played for the Chicago Bears. More than 70,000 fans came to watch the Giants play the Bears. New fans fell in love with the sport. The Giants have been popular ever since.

Many fans wanted to see Red Grange (with ball) and the Chicago Bears play the Giants in New York on December 6, 1925.

WHO THEY PLAY

The New York Giants play 16 games each season. With so few games, each one is important. Every year, the Giants play two games against each of the other three teams in their division. Those teams are the Philadelphia Eagles, Washington Redskins, and Dallas Cowboys. The Giants also play six other teams from the NFC and four from the AFC. The Giants have played the Eagles more than 160 times. Philadelphia is only about 100 miles from New York. That keeps the **rivalry** strong.

The Giants and the Philadelphia Eagles have been battling since 1933.

WHERE THEY PLAY

The Giants have shared homes with two New York baseball teams and the New York Jets football team. They even played at the Yale Bowl in Connecticut for two seasons. The Giants started playing in Giants Stadium in 1976. The Jets moved in in 1984. Then in 2010, MetLife Stadium opened in New Jersey. It holds 82,500 people. The Giants and Jets share it. The stadium hosted the Super Bowl after the 2013 season.

The Seattle Seahawks beat the Denver Broncos 43-8 in the Super Bowl on February 2, 2014, at MetLife Stadium.

THE FOOTBALL FIELD

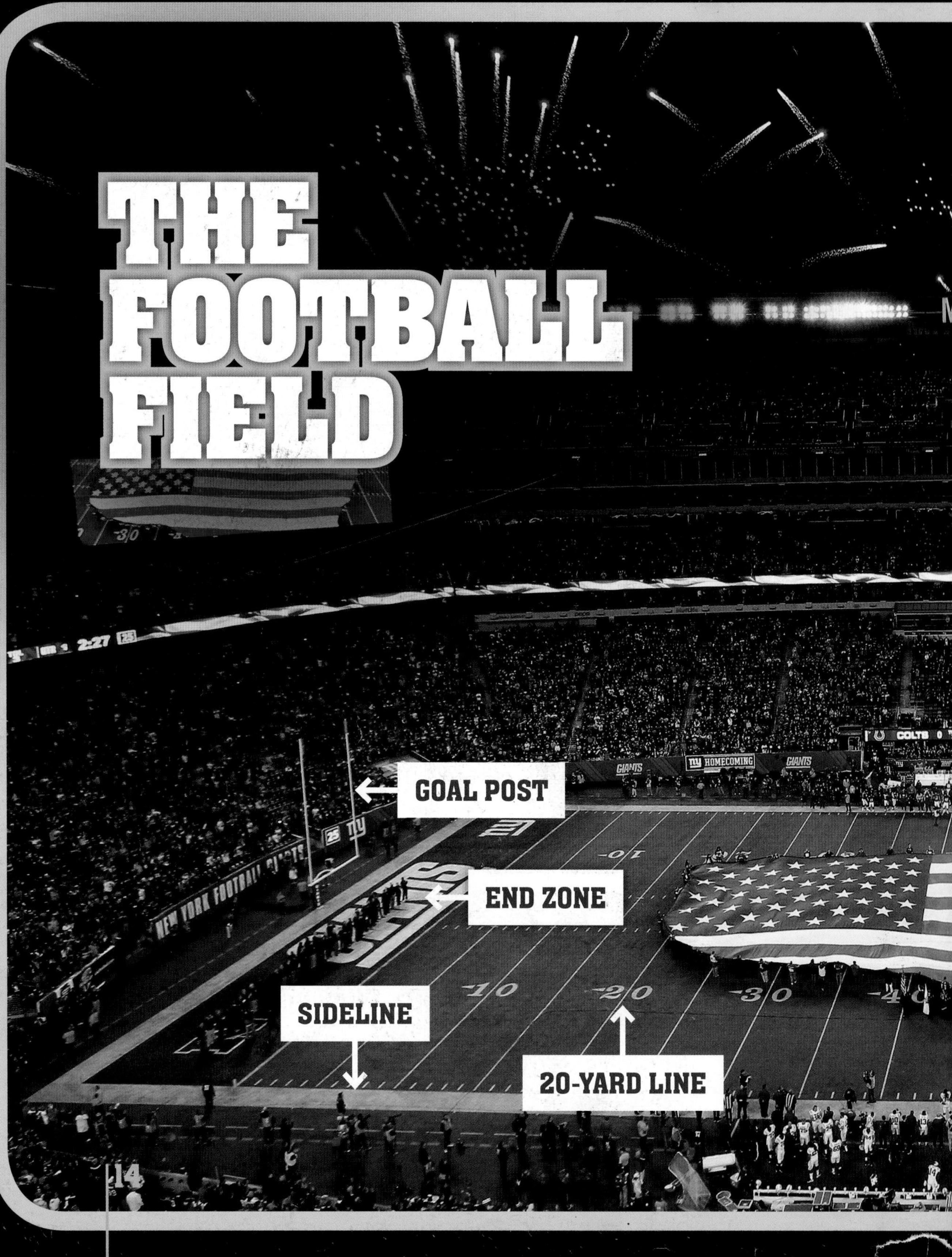

GOAL POST

END ZONE

SIDELINE

20-YARD LINE

FE STADIUM

END LINE ←

HASH MARKS ↓

GOAL LINE →

BENCH AREA ↓

BIG DAYS

The Giants have had some great moments in their history. Here are three of the greatest:

1934—The Giants met the Chicago Bears for the NFL title. The field in New York was frozen. Both teams slid around in the first half. The Bears stayed in their cleats. But the Giants switched to sneakers at halftime to get better traction. The Giants won "The Sneakers Game" 30-13.

1983—The Giants had made the playoffs once in 19 years. Then the team hired Bill Parcells as coach. He had never coached in the NFL. Parcells made the defense strong. He led the Giants to two Super Bowl titles in eight years.

Coach Bill Parcells is carried off the field after the Giants' 20-19 Super Bowl win on January 27, 1991.

2008—The 2007 Giants barely made the playoffs. But then they won three straight playoff games. They made it to the Super Bowl on February 3. There they met the undefeated New England Patriots. The Patriots had set scoring records that season. But New York scored a **touchdown** with 35 seconds left to win the Super Bowl 17-14.

TOUGH DAYS

Football is a hard game. Even the best teams have rough games and seasons. Here are some of the toughest times in Giants history:

1947—New York had finished second in the NFL in 1946. But things got bad quickly. The next year, the Giants had the worst record in the league. New York finished 2-8-2.

1974—The Giants played home games in New Haven, Connecticut, while waiting for their new stadium to be built. Fans were angry. They did not want to make the long drive to New Haven. The team lost every game there and went 2-12.

Linebacker Lawrence Taylor sits in the locker room after the Giants' loss to the New York Jets in the final game of the 1988 season.

1988—The Giants had 10 wins with one game to go. All they had to do was beat the New York Jets to make the playoffs. The Jets were not very good. But they scored a touchdown with 37 seconds left to beat the Giants 27-21.

MEET THE FANS

New York fans have a nickname for the Giants. They call the team "Big Blue" because of the team's colors. The Giants sell out most of their home games. Fans even show up in the freezing New Jersey weather. Unlike most teams, the Giants do not have cheerleaders or a mascot. But fans still get loud to support the Giants.

Giants fans celebrate with safety Kenny Phillips after a playoff win over the Green Bay Packers on January 15, 2012.

HEROES THEN

Frank Gifford led the Giants to the 1956 title. He was named **Most Valuable Player (MVP)**. Gifford made the **Pro Bowl** at three different positions during his career. Lawrence Taylor is one of the best linebackers ever. He used his speed to **sack** quarterbacks. Taylor became known for the strip-sack. He would knock down the quarterback and force a fumble at the same time. Defensive end Michael Strahan was also a sack master. He set the single-season record with 22.5 sacks in 2001.

Defensive end Michael Strahan was one of the best pass rushers of all time.

HEROES NOW

Quarterback Eli Manning led New York to two Super Bowl **upsets** over the New England Patriots. He was named MVP of both games. Defensive end Jason Pierre-Paul is a strong pass rusher. He had 16.5 sacks in the team's 2011 championship season. Wide receiver Victor Cruz averaged 80 catches in his first three seasons as a starter. Fans love his salsa dance touchdown celebration. Odell Beckham Jr. is another great wide receiver. He is fast and acrobatic. Beckham Jr. was a rookie in 2014. He played in just 12 games that season. But he still finished in the NFL's top ten in receptions, receiving yards, and receiving touchdowns.

Wide receiver Victor Cruz does his salsa dance celebration after scoring a touchdown against the Houston Texans on September 21, 2014.

GEARING UP

NFL players wear team uniforms. They wear helmets and pads to keep them safe. Cleats help them make quick moves and run fast. Some players wear extra gear for protection.

THE FOOTBALL

NFL footballs are made of leather. Under the leather is a lining that fills with air to give the ball its shape. The leather has bumps or "pebbles." These help players grip the ball. Laces help players control their throws. Footballs are also called "pigskins" because some of the first balls were made from pig bladders. Today they are made of leather from cows.

Eli Manning prepares to throw during a game against the Atlanta Falcons on December 16, 2012.

HELMET

SHOULDER PADS

THIGH PADS

FOOTBALL

CLEATS

27

SPORTS STATS

ere are some of the all-time career records for the New York Giants. All the stats are through the 2014 season.

RUSHING YARDS

Tiki Barber 10,449

Rodney Hampton 6,897

RECEPTIONS

Amani Toomer 668

Tiki Barber 586

PASSING YARDS

Eli Manning 39,755

Phil Simms 33,462

INTERCEPTIONS

Emlen Tunnell 74

Jimmy Patton 52

SACKS

Michael Strahan 141.5

Lawrence Taylor 132.5

POINTS

Pete Gogolak 646

Lawrence Tynes 586

Running back Tiki Barber was great at running and catching the ball out of the backfield.

TOTAL TOUCHDOWNS

Frank Gifford 78

Tiki Barber 68

GLOSSARY

league an organization of sports teams that compete against each other

Most Valuable Player (MVP) a yearly award given to the top player in the NFL

Pro Bowl the NFL's All-Star game where the best players in the league compete

rivalry an ongoing competition between teams that play each other often, over a long time

sack when the quarterback is tackled behind the line of scrimmage before he can throw the ball

Super Bowl the championship game of the NFL, played between the winners of the AFC and the NFC

touchdown a play in which the ball is held in the other team's end zone, resulting in six points

upsets when a supposedly weaker team beats a supposedly stronger team

FIND OUT MORE

IN THE LIBRARY

Frisch, Aaron. *Super Bowl Champions: New York Giants*. San Francisco: Chronicle Books, 2014.

Scheff, Matt. *Superstars Of The New York Giants*. Mankato, MN: Amicus High Interest, 2013.

Wyner, Zach. *Inside The NFL: New York Giants*. New York: Av2, 2014.

ON THE WEB

Visit our Web site for links about the New York Giants:
childsworld.com/links

Note to Parents, Teachers, and Librarians: We routinely verify our Web links to make sure they are safe and active sites. So encourage your readers to check them out!

INDEX